BIBLE FACTS ABOUT

HEAVEN

SWEET HOME OF DEPARTED SAINTS

JOHN R. RICE

". . .a precious unfolding of truth concerning the Father's House, designed to comfort the hearts of those who have been bereaved and to stir others with a desire to know the One whose presence makes Heaven, that they may be with Him forever in eternity. There are 8 chapters, and every one clear and scriptural. An ideal book for ministers to put into the hands of those who are mourning the loss of Christian friends and relatives."

—H. A. Ironside

SWORD of the LORD
PUBLISHERS
P.O.BOX 1099, MURFREESBORO, TN 37133

Printed in U.S.A.

Presented to _____

By _____

With prayer that God may use this message to comfort you and bless your heart with the message of Heaven, the beautiful prepared place not far away to which Jesus will take all who trust themselves to Him to save and keep.

Table of Contents

VI. CHRISTIAN, "TO DIE IS GAIN"; WE SHOULD LONG FOR HEAVEN

Many Christians act like heathens at funerals. "Blessed are the dead which die in the Lord." What a Christian gains at death: the presence of Christ, seeing loved ones again, being done with sin, no more sinful companions, hearts comforted, rest, eternal rewards.

VII. CHRIST MAY COME TODAY TO TAKE HIS OWN

The hope of a Christian is not death but the second coming. "I will come again, and receive you unto myself." His coming is imminent. Christians are to watch continually, expectantly. The joy of going to Heaven without dying.

VIII. CHRIST THE WAY TO HEAVEN; MAKE SURE YOU ARE GOING THERE

What men have done in hope of gaining Heaven. Jesus the only way; how Christ paid for sins; how He invites sinners. All who receive and trust Him for salvation are sure of Heaven. How to meet loved ones there. A decision to make today.

How to Use This Booklet

First, enjoy it. Saints of old rejoiced as they talked about Heaven. Their songs were about Heaven. And Jesus commanded His disciples, "Rejoice, because your names are written in heaven" (Luke 10:20).

Pray God to make Heaven real to you. It is not far away. Angels go and come continually from Heaven to earth and back. Heavenly beings watch us with infinite tenderness. They rejoice when a sinner repents.

Search out the Scriptures. Carefully check every reference. Let no unbelief steal away your joy in the blessed promises about Heaven.

If this message can make Heaven real and sweet to you, it will have been well worthwhile.

In Mississippi I sat late talking to two old saints of God about the Lord and the happy land to which they would soon be going. As we talked, prayed and praised the Lord together, Heaven seemed very near.

The next day as I drove five hundred miles, from Mississippi across Louisiana and part of Texas, I dictated to Miss Viola most of this book. It was sweet to my soul and I trust will be sweet to yours.

Next, use this booklet to comfort people. Multitudes who have lost loved ones by death are anxious to know where they are and whether they will meet them again. Oh, if they knew what is in the Bible about Heaven, how much lighter it would make their burdens!

Great peace can God's message about Heaven give to a troubled heart, so give them this book and earnestly pray that God will make Heaven real to them. Earth has no sorrow that Heaven cannot heal.

Some are old, sick and troubled. This world loses its appeal when the steps become tottering, the hearing becomes dim, and failing eyes don't see as they once did. With loved ones gone, riches or fame or pleasure become baubles and trash. Give old people this book to comfort their hearts and lighten their way.

Some are sick with an incurable disease and have not much time. They would rejoice in the good news about a far country which after all is not very far, a place where the Saviour has promised to take them if they trust Him.

Put this booklet in the hands of old, sorrowing, sick, the troubled. By talking to them about Heaven, Jesus comforted the apostles the night before Gethsemane's burden and before Calvary's awful sacrifice. Even on the cross He talked to the dying thief about the Paradise to which He would take him that very day.

Third, use this booklet to win souls. Many times hearts have grown tender as they found the sweet provision God has made in Heaven for those who will trust Him. The message of Heaven is a soul-winning message. Jesus told the doubting and troubled disciples, "I am the way, the truth, and the life: no man cometh unto the Father, but by me." Jesus is the way to Heaven. So use this booklet to get many saved.

At the close is a decision form, making it easy for readers to write down their names in a solemn transaction of trusting Jesus Christ for salvation and claiming Him open-ly. The decision must be made in the heart, but it will help to give assurance and honor God if it is made more definite and more public by a solemn, signed agree-ment. This decision slip may make it easier for some to see how simple it is to trust in Jesus Christ for salvation.

Prayerfully use it, and make sure that it is not a mere form but an honest action of a heart in full surrender and trust, giving over the whole heart, life and soul to Jesus Christ.

And now, dear reader, if you love the Lord Jesus and have trusted Him as Saviour, then one glad day I will meet you in the Homeland, in the Father's house of many mansions; and there together we will sing redemption's song and worship Him forever.

1—The Comfort of Heaven

"Let not your heart be troubled: ye believe in God, believe also in me. In my Father's house are many mansions: if it were not so, I would have told you. I go to prepare a place for you. And if I go and prepare a place for you, I will come again, and receive you unto myself; that where I am, there ye may be also. And whither I go ye know, and the way ye know. Thomas saith unto him, Lord, we know not whither thou goest; and how can we know the way? Jesus saith unto him, I am the way, the truth, and the life: no man cometh unto the Father, but by me."—John 14:1-6.

Heaven was so real to many of the saints of ages past.

> Oh, sing to me of Heaven
> When I am called to die,

they sang. I can remember in my youth hearing Christians sing with tears streaming down their faces:

> I have a mother over yonder,
> I have a mother over yonder,
> I have a mother over yonder
> On the other bright shore.
>
> Some glad day I'll go and meet her,
> Some glad day I'll go and meet her,
> Some glad day I'll go and meet her
> On the other bright shore.

It was sung many times in little churches as people went from one to another shaking hands—sung while tears of joy ran down faces. Other verses were: "I have a father over yonder" or brother or sister, and last of all, "I have a Saviour over yonder." It was very real to them.

> There'll be no sorrow there,
> There'll be no sorrow there.
> In Heaven above, where all is love,
> There'll be no sorrow there

was a song mother sang. Its memory is sweet. The saints of God seemed to 'stand on Jordan's stormy banks and cast a wishful eye to Canaan's fair and happy land, where their possessions lie.'

To many, the last stanza of the old hymn written by Samuel Stennett seemed to express a sincere heart longing:

> When shall I reach that happy place,
> And be forever blest?
> When shall I see my Father's face,
> And in His bosom rest?

People sang many songs about Heaven. "In the Sweet By and By," "When We All Get to Heaven," "Oh, Come, Angel Band," the magnificent "Glory Song" sung around the world in the Torrey-Alexander meetings, had their tremendous hold on people, no doubt because of the happy hope they expressed for Heaven. The human heart longs for an assurance of a blessed, immortal place where the good, the forgiven, the blessed are at home with God; when sin, disappointment, human failure, heartache, disease and death are forever ended!

It seems that in recent years there has been more con-fusion in people's minds about Heaven and less under-standing of the Bible doctrine concerning that glorious place. For one thing, isms and false cults have increased to confuse the mind. Then there has been a great decrease in preaching about death, Hell, Heaven and judgment. Modernism and worldliness have discouraged the flabby, soft-living hirelings of the pulpit from preaching about death and what follows.

But you cannot dismiss Hell without dismissing Heaven. You cannot ignore or evade the fate of the unrepentant sinner and teach the saints the glories that await the redeemed of God. The so-called "social gospel" lays stress upon this life, not on the next. In many quarters it is now regarded as very old-fashioned and passe' to urge people to prepare to die. Social security, better housing, relief for tenant farmers, better living conditions for the poor and the care of underprivileged children—these have occupied so much of the teaching and preaching of these modern days that preachers have left hungry-hearted people ignorant about Heaven.

We ought to think and preach about Heaven far more than we do. Saints should rejoice because their names are written in Heaven and should think of the joy in Heaven over one sinner that repents. Sinners should be continually warned that they will miss the eternal joys and glories of Heaven and will, like the rich man, lift up their eyes in Hell, being in torment, if they do not repent.

This world is only an anteroom of the next. This short life is incidental compared with eternity. This world is not home to the Christian. Here we are only sojourners, temporary dwellers in a foreign land. Our citizenship is in Heaven. Our treasure should be in Heaven. Our thoughts should dwell lovingly and longingly on that sweet home of the departed saints, of our Saviour and of our Heavenly Father.

2—Heaven, a Real, Literal Place

When Jesus sent Judas away from the upper room with the words, "That thou doest, do quickly," and Satan entered into Judas so that he, burning with hate, went to the chief priests to betray Jesus for thirty pieces of silver; and when Jesus finally convinced the eleven remaining disciples that He was to be crucified the next day, it was the darkest hour any of them ever saw! In numbed misery, they huddled near Jesus. Beyond a doubt, there seemed only an unknown blackness. Misery and death filled their hearts. So to comfort them, the Saviour told them:

"In my Father's house are many mansions: if it were not so, I would have told you. I go to prepare a PLACE for you. And if I go and prepare a PLACE for you, I will come again, and receive you unto myself; that where I am, there ye may be also."—John 14:2,3.

So Heaven is a PLACE. Twice Jesus called it that. He has gone to prepare this place. It is in the Father's house of many mansions. We do not know how the darkened minds of the eleven disciples reacted to this comforting word: 'Let not your heart be troubled because there is a heavenly place with many mansions in the Father's house.' Doubtless the Saviour, facing the torments of Gethsemane, His betrayal, His desertion by the disciples, His trial before the Sanhedrin and Pilate, and the agonies of the cross, was Himself sweetly comforted by remembering the happy place to which He was going and where He would prepare many mansions for His own redeemed. Certain it is that countless millions have learned not to let their hearts be troubled as the sweet realization of Heaven as an actual place has come home to their hearts.

Don't think of Heaven as a ghostly, unreal, indefinite state. It is a real place, a place as literal and concrete as the house you sit in today, as physically real as the city where you live. Human telescopes cannot see on what distant planet or star is the Paradise of God, where, in the tabernacle of God with its streets of gold and gates of pearl, Jesus is preparing many mansions. But though human eyes are too dim to reach it, it is there—a physical place.

Revelation 21 and 22 tell us something of this wonderful place that Jesus is preparing for His saints, "the holy city," "that great city, the holy Jerusalem." Oh, the shining brightness of it! "Having the glory of God; and her light was like unto a stone most precious, even like a jasper stone, clear as crystal"! It is a literal city with walls of shining jasper, 144 cubits high. The streets are pure gold, and the foundations of the wall of the city are decorated with every kind of precious stone. The city has twelve great gates, each one a pearl.

The wonderful city is 12,000 furlongs square. There are ten furlongs to an English mile (eight to a Roman mile); so that city far surpasses all the cities of earth in size. It is 1500 miles long, 1500 miles wide, and 1500 miles high. Oh, the gleaming beauty of that wonderful place!

A river runs through the city, coming out from the throne of God and of Christ. And on each side of the river are the trees of life which bear twelve kinds of fruit and bring forth their fruit every month and whose leaves are healing leaves—for the healing of the nations. The river is the pure water of life without a germ and without a stain, but clear as crystal!

No doubt we saints of God will eat the fruit and drink the water in real bodies. Our feet will walk upon those streets. Our hands will touch the cheeks of our loved ones. Our arms will embrace them again. Every longing will be satisfied.

I tell you, Heaven is a real, literal, physical place, a city as material, as physical, as literal as Chicago or London or New York or Tokyo.

The Saviour said He was going to prepare us a place. How wonderful it will be is beyond human computation. Remember that in six days Christ made the heavens and earth and all that in them is. "Without him was not any thing made that was made" (John 1:3).

If He made so many wonders in six days, then what beauties and marvels He has surely prepared during these 1900 years in which He has been preparing our mansions in the Father's House!

Where is Heaven? Up, somewhere away from this planet. Jesus went *up* to Heaven. "While they beheld, he was taken *up*" (Acts 1:9). "Elijah went *up* by a whirlwind into heaven" (II Kings 2:11). Even when Paul received special revelations, he was "caught *up* to the third heaven" (II Cor. 12:2) and "caught *up* into paradise" (II Cor. 12:4). At least Paul knew such an one, and I believe that it was Paul himself.

Heaven is UP. Somewhere out in space God has His beautiful holy city, the house of many mansions, with its shining walls, streets of pure gold, its river of life, its trees with twelve kinds of fruit, and where there is no night.

But for the Christian, Heaven will be where Christ is. He is now there with the Father, but one day He will come and get us and take us away to those heavenly mansions.

Then after a honeymoon in Heaven, Christ will come to reign on the earth. The angel told Mary, "The Lord God shall give unto him the throne of his father David: And he shall reign over the house of Jacob for ever; and of his kingdom there shall be no end" (Luke 1:32,33). And Matthew 25:31 tells us, "When the Son of man shall come in his glory, and all the holy angels with him, then shall he sit upon the throne of his glory."

When the Lord comes to reign on the earth, His saints will come with Him. In I Thessalonians 4:13-18, concerning the coming of Christ and the raising of the Christian dead, the promise closes with these words: "And so shall we ever be with the Lord. Wherefore comfort one another with these words." Where Jesus goes, we will go.

When He reigns on the earth, we shall reign with Him. In Revelation 5:10 we hear the praises of redeemed saints in Heaven saying that Christ "hast made us unto our God kings and priests: and we shall reign on the earth." The Scripture says, "If we suffer, we shall also reign with him" (II Tim. 2:12). Revelation 20:6 says, "Blessed and holy is he that hath part in the first resurrection: on such the second death hath no power, but they shall be priests of God and of Christ, and shall reign with him a thousand years."

So for a thousand years Heaven for the Christian is going to be on earth. That happy reign of Christ is pictured in Isaiah 11:1-16 and in Micah, chapter 4.

Then—

"The wolf also shall dwell with the lamb, and the leopard shall lie down with the kid; and the calf and the young lion and the fatling together; and a little child shall lead them. And the cow and the bear shall feed; their young ones shall lie down together: and the lion shall eat straw like the ox. And the sucking child shall play on the hole of the asp, and the weaned child shall put his hand on the cockatrice' den. They shall not hurt nor destroy in all my holy mountain: for the earth shall be full of the knowledge of the Lord, as the waters cover the sea."—Isa. 11:6-9.

There will be peace and joy on earth when Christ will reign as King of kings and Lord of lords. Then the nations "shall beat their swords into plowshares, and their spears into pruninghooks: nation shall not lift up a sword against nation, neither shall they learn war any more" (Mic. 4:3). Nations shall serve the true God in peace and holiness.

"Then the eyes of the blind shall be opened, and the ears of the deaf shall be unstopped. Then shall the lame man leap as an hart, and the tongue of the dumb sing. . . . And the ransomed of the Lord shall return, and come to Zion with songs and everlasting joy upon their heads: they shall obtain joy and gladness, and sorrow and sighing shall flee away."—Isa. 35:5,6,10.

At the end of the thousand years the last sinner will be judged, the earth forever will be purged by fire of all the taint of sin; then the New Jerusalem will come down from God out of Heaven—that "Father's house" of many mansions, that "Tabernacle of God"—and Heaven will consist of this wonderful city on a new earth, surrounded by a new firmament. Then there will be no need for light, for the Lord God and the Lamb shall be the light of it! And there will be no night there.

Then "he will dwell with them, and they shall be his people, and God himself shall be with them, and be their God. And God shall wipe away all tears from their eyes; and there shall be no more death, neither sorrow, nor crying, neither shall there be any more pain: for the former things are passed away" (Rev. 21:3,4).

Then in Heaven, "his servants shall serve him: And they shall see his face; and his name shall be in their foreheads. And there shall be no night there; and they need no candle, neither light of the sun; for the Lord God giveth them light: and they shall reign for ever and ever" (Rev. 22:3-5).

Oh, may God make Heaven real to us! It is a real place, a physical, literal place prepared for us by the Saviour.

We must remember that Jesus went to Heaven with a physical body. His body came out of Joseph's new tomb. To His astonished disciples who were afraid when they saw Him, Jesus said, "A spirit hath not flesh and bones, as ye see me have." He said, "It is I myself: handle me, and see" (Luke 24:39). He invited poor, doubting Thomas to "reach hither thy finger, and behold my hands; and reach hither thy hand, and thrust it into my side: and be not faithless, but believing" (John 20:27). Later, in writing of Him, John the beloved spoke of Jesus as the One "which . . .our hands have handled" (I John 1:1). Long later, when the resurrected and glorified Jesus met the aged John on the isle of Patmos and gave him The Revelation, Jesus laid His physical hand upon the head of John. I say, Jesus has a physical body, a body of flesh and bones, a body of material substance.

When Jesus ascended to Heaven from the mount of Olives, there stood by the disciples two men in white apparel which said, "Ye men of Galilee, why stand ye gazing up into heaven? this same Jesus, which is taken up from you into heaven, shall so come in like manner as ye have seen him go into heaven" (Acts 1:11).

Note that they said, "THIS SAME JESUS. . . ." The Jesus in Heaven is not another but the same. The Jesus who will return for His saints is not another but the same. When He comes again to Jerusalem, Jews will look on Him whom they have pierced (Zech. 12:10). They will ask, "What are these wounds in thine hands?" He will answer, "Those with which I was wounded in the house of my friends" (Zech. 13:6). His feet shall stand in that day upon the mount of Olives (Zech. 14:4). Jesus now has hands and feet, the same with which He went away, hands and feet with the marks of nails! And this same Jesus now abides in Heaven with a physical body. I tell you, Heaven must be and is a real, literal, physical place!

In Heaven Enoch has a physical body. He never died. Rather, we are told, "Enoch walked with God: and he was not; for God took him" (Gen. 5:24).

Hebrews 11:5 tells us, "By faith Enoch was translated that he should not see death; and was not found, because God had translated him."

People may have looked for his body, but he "was not found," for the body was translated, taken literally and physically to Heaven. Since the body of Enoch did not die, then it must still be alive. Since his body was not found on earth, then it was taken immediately to Heaven.

And this verse says Enoch went straight to Heaven where God is. God did not SEND Enoch anywhere but TOOK him. Enoch, in his physical body, was taken where God is, and is in that happy home of God, angels and departed saints!

The Scriptures tell us that on the insistence of doubters, fifty men for three days scoured the country, trying to find Elijah's body. It was not on earth but had gone to Heaven. The physical body of Elijah is in Heaven.

The Bible makes clear that Elijah, in a living human body, did not go down into the earth, but "Elijah went up by a whirlwind into heaven" (II Kings 2:11). He was taken "into heaven." As the Lord TOOK Enoch, so God twice says the Lord would "take away" Elijah (II Kings 2:3,5).

Of all the race of mankind, the only two that we know definitely went to Heaven without dying were Enoch and Elijah. They were translated while yet alive and physically transferred to Heaven. With chariot and horses of fire, Elijah was carried to Heaven in a whirlwind. Therefore, we know there are at least three beings in Heaven with physical bodies—Jesus, Enoch and Elijah.

The bodies of Enoch and Elijah are not "resurrected" since they never died. In I Corinthians 15:20 we read, "Now is Christ risen from the dead, and become the firstfruits of them that slept." Christ is the first ever to be raised physically from the dead and given a glorified body. But when Christ returned to Heaven with His glorified body, Enoch and Elijah were already there in their physical bodies.

When Jesus arose from the dead and came from the grave with His glorious body, a body with hands and feet, a body which the disciples could handle and feel, a body which ate and drank before them, many other bodies likewise came from the graves. Matthew 27:52,53 says, "And the graves were opened; and many bodies of the saints which slept arose, And came out of the graves after his resurrection, and went into the holy city, and appeared unto many."

Note that this speaks of BODIES, literal, physical bodies. Many Bible scholars think these bodies went straight to Heaven. In the Scofield Reference Bible, Dr. C. I. Scofield says:

> That these bodies returned to their graves is not said and may not be inferred. The wave-sheaf (Lev. 23:10-12) typifies the resurrection of Christ, but a sheaf implies plurality. It was a single "corn of wheat" that fell into the ground in the crucifixion and entombment of Christ (John 12:24); it was a sheaf which came forth in resurrection. The inference is that these saints. . .went with Jesus (Eph. 4:8-10) into heaven.

So in Heaven there may be many with their physical bodies, bodies of flesh and bone, hands and feet, bodies just as real as they had on earth.

It is at least possible, perhaps probable, that even the others in Heaven are temporarily clothed with some kind of human bodies, awaiting the resurrection of their own. As to that, we cannot say. However, we do know that, when Moses appeared on the Mount of Transfiguration with Elijah to talk with Jesus, he appeared visibly in the sight of the disciples. "And there appeared unto them Elias with Moses: and they were talking with Jesus" (Mark 9:4). Moses, who had died and whose body had been buried by the angel of God (Deut. 34:5,6), appeared visibly to the disciples.

When Samuel was called back from the dead, he

appeared visibly to Saul and to the witch of Endor (I Sam. 28:12).

In Hell the rich man SAW Abraham and SAW Lazarus in his bosom (Luke 16:23).

John SAW "under the altar the souls of them that were slain for the word of God, and for the testimony which they held" (Rev. 6:9). If the souls now in Heaven do not have physical bodies, they certainly appeared visibly to men.

Yes—Heaven is a real, physical place, as concrete and literal as the city in which you live, with physical properties and dimensions, made of material substance, praise God! And Jesus is there preparing real mansions for His redeemed so that, where He is, we may be also. Hallelujah!

3—Heaven Immediately Follows Death for Christians

Among many unscriptural doctrines invented by Roman Catholic church leaders is that of purgatory or limbo. Catholics believe that at death the souls of ordinary Christians descend to purgatory. Loved ones of the departed are taught that they should pay the priest to say masses for the dead and pray for the souls in purgatory. Eventually, if enough masses are said and prayers uttered, the soul may pass from purgatory into Heaven.

But that is not taught in the Bible. It is based on a doctrine of salvation by works and by the church instead of redemption by the blood of Christ. It is used to extort money from those who hope to shorten the period of suffering of their loved ones that they may the sooner enter Heaven.

But not one word in the Bible indicates that anybody at death goes to an intermediate state between Heaven and Hell. The terms "purgatory" and "limbo" are not found in the Word of God, nor is any other term of similar meaning.

There are others who teach soul-sleeping. They think that at the death of a Christian, the soul is put to sleep and does not waken until the resurrection of the Christian's body. Perhaps that idea arose from the Bible use of the word *sleep* for the death of a Christian. In I Thessalonians 4:14 God says that, at the coming of Christ to raise the Christian dead and receive the Christian living to Himself, "Them also which sleep in Jesus will God bring with him." It is said of Stephen that "he fell asleep" at his death (Acts 7:60).

However, only the body sleeps. The body rests. Those mortal, physical eyes do not see nor the ears hear nor the tongue speak nor the brain know. The bodies of saints are asleep, safe in the arms of Jesus our Lord who will raise them up at His coming. Many Scriptures make clear that the soul does not sleep at death. Death for the Christian is not oblivion, not darkness, not forgetfulness, but the entering in of a bright new day of perfect and glorious life.

Sweet assurance of this truth is given. In Luke 23:39-43 we see how the repenting thief turned to Jesus on the cross beside him and said, "Lord, remember me when thou comest into thy kingdom."

No doubt he had in mind the truth so clearly taught in the Old Testament, that the Messiah would sit on David's throne at Jerusalem and reign over Israel in Palestine. When the Saviour was promised to Mary, the Angel Gabriel

said, "The Lord God shall give unto him the throne of
his father David: And he shall reign over the house of
Jacob for ever; and of his kingdom there shall be no
end" (Luke 1:32,33). Jesus is now seated on His Father's
throne (Rev. 3:21). But "When the Son of man shall come
in his glory, and all the holy angels with him, then shall
he sit upon the throne of his glory" (Matt. 25:31).

The dying thief confessed that he had made an utter
failure of his life. Acknowledging his sin and appealing
to Jesus as the Lord, he begged, "Remember me. . ."!
This criminal knew little about Heaven, but he knew
about the promised kingdom of Christ the Messiah.

With loving forgiveness, Jesus turned to the penitent
sinner and promised salvation not only in the distant
day of His kingdom but "to day," said Jesus, "shalt thou
be with me in paradise." That very day the dying thief
entered into the Paradise of God with Jesus or, in the
term to which we are accustomed, entered Heaven
that day.

There are those who believe that Paradise and Heaven
are not the same, but we think they are mistaken. On
the cross Jesus said, "Father, into thy hands I commend
my spirit" (Luke 23:46). He went to be with the Father,
and the dying thief went with Him that very day into
Heaven!

The Apostles' Creed, quoted by many, states that Jesus
died and "descended into hell." In the English language
that statement is misleading. When Psalm 16:10 says,
"Thou wilt not leave my soul in hell" (speaking about
Jesus), it literally means that God would not leave the
spirit of Jesus in the place of the dead, a very general
term which included both Heaven and Hell under the

Hebrew word *sheol*, simply meaning the unseen state or the place of the dead. The Father received Christ's spirit and that of the dying thief the very day they died.

"Enoch walked with God: and he was not; for God took him." In simple language, Enoch went to Heaven. God took him, so Enoch went to be with God at once.

When Elijah went to Heaven, he, like Enoch, took his body with him. He went at once, without any sleeping of soul, any intermediate state. "And it came to pass, as they still went on, and talked, that, behold, there appeared a chariot of fire, and horses of fire, and parted them both asunder; and Elijah went up by a whirlwind into heaven" (II Kings 2:11).

Jesus gives an even clearer teaching that the soul of a Christian at death goes immediately to Heaven and that the soul of the unconverted goes immediately to torment. In Luke 16:19-31 a rich man is pictured who fared sumptuously every day, and a beggar named Lazarus laid at his gate full of sores. "The beggar died, and was carried by the angels into Abraham's bosom," Jesus said. "The rich man also died, and was buried; and in hell he lift up his eyes, being in torments."

The real Lazarus (not that poor, frail, diseased body, but his spirit) was carried by the angels of God straight home to Heaven where Abraham was. Christ revealed the conversation that took place between Abraham in Heaven and the rich man in Hell immediately after Lazarus and the rich man died. No soul-sleeping there, no purgatory either, for the words of Abraham to the rich man are given: "And beside all this, between us and you there is a great gulf fixed: so that they which would pass from hence to you cannot; neither can they pass to us, that would come from thence."

Paul said in II Corinthians 5:8, "We are confident, I say, and willing rather to be absent from the body, and to be present with the Lord."

Every saint who is absent from the body is present with the Lord Jesus in Heaven. At death the soul of the Christian is carried by the angels of God straight Home where Christ and the Father are.

4—Christians Know Each Other in Heaven

Does personality extend beyond the grave? Do those we love retain those definite, personal characteristics by which we may know them when they go to be with the Lord and leave these bodies of clay? We answer with perfect assurance: Yes!

Whatever we have left of human weakness and sin will surely be left behind when at death the soul finds itself in the likeness of Christ. We shall lose whatever remains of the carnal and sinful nature, while our personalities will remain. The imperfect will be made perfect. The incomplete will be completed. That which is lacking will be supplied.

Yet those who rejoice in the presence of Christ will be as their loved ones knew them here on earth. The Abraham who was on earth is still Abraham, but in Heaven! Lazarus, the poor beggar, was sick; now he is well. He was a beggar; now he is rich. He was in pain; now he is comforted. Yet he is the same Lazarus and was instantly recognized by the rich man who looked up from Hell.

Do the saints in Heaven know each other? Assuredly

they do! In I Corinthians 13:12 the Holy Spirit gives us this inspired statement: "For now we see through a glass, darkly; but then face to face: now I know in part; but then shall I know even as also I am known."

In Heaven they know each other better than people ever know each other on earth. On the earth "man looketh on the outward appearance, but the Lord looketh on the heart" (I Sam. 16:7).

Dear friends and loved ones here often misunderstand us, not knowing the desires and motives of our hearts. We misjudge because we can see only through a glass darkly. We may see faces, we may hear words, but how imperfectly these reveal the heart within!

No one can look at a friend and judge rightly whether he lies or speaks the truth. Many a time a mother, a father, a wife, a sweetheart, yearns in vain to express the love that is humanly past expressing. Only in Heaven shall we really know how some people love us. Only in Heaven shall we know how deep was the penitence of others for sin and how desperately people longed to do right, though they appeared not to try. Here we see through a glass darkly; then we shall see face to face.

In Heaven not only shall we know those we knew on earth, but we shall know others. No one will need to introduce me to Paul, to David, to good Barnabas, to the martyr Stephen or to sweet Mary!

The disciples recognized Moses and Elijah on the Mount of Transfiguration. The rich man in Hell recognized Lazarus and Abraham when he saw them together in Heaven.

People in the next world—both the saved in Heaven and the lost in Hell—retain all their senses. Though their bodies are yet in the grave, they see as if they had eyes, hear as if they had ears, speak as if they had tongues and lips. The rich man in torment SAW Abraham and Lazarus in Paradise. They HEARD one another speak. The rich man FELT the torment of Hell. Lazarus was COMFORTED as sensibly as the rich man was tormented.

We ignorantly think that the eye sees. It does not. It is the soul that sees, using the eyes for windows. Human, physical ears do not hear. They are merely the physical instruments which the soul can use while clothed in these physical bodies. But the soul can hear without ears. We say that the tongue speaks: it is not the tongue but the person behind the tongue that speaks.

These organs of clay in the human body have no senses when their master, the soul, is departed. God is a Spirit, yet "the EYES of the Lord run to and fro throughout the whole earth, to shew himself strong in the behalf of them whose heart is perfect toward him" (II Chron. 16:9). God is a Spirit, yet the voice of God spoke from Mount Sinai "all these words" (Exod. 20:1).

I say, in Heaven our loved ones who have gone to be with Christ see, hear, speak, sing, rejoice! Life is fuller, richer, more glorious, more real with the saints in Glory than with the saints on earth.

After we have received the witness of the Scriptures, it is sweet to remember the testimony of a multitude of dying saints. How many times some Spirit-filled Christian on a deathbed has rejoiced, has heard the singing of angels, has seen the Lord Jesus and saints gone on before! When dying Stephen, filled with the Holy Spirit, saw Jesus standing on the right hand of God in Heaven, he said, "Lord Jesus, receive my spirit." That was not hallucination; that was real. Before he died, Stephen actually saw Jesus Christ and said so.

How well I remember when my mother lay dying. Around the room her husband, children and kin looked on and wept while she urged each to promise to meet her in Heaven. We did promise we would. Though less than six years old, I remember how mother asked my cousin to sing and play

> How firm a foundation
> Ye saints of the Lord,
> Is laid for your faith
> In His excellent Word!

Mother rested wholly on the Rock that day, and it did not tremble beneath her dying feet! Mother walked through the valley of shadow that day and feared no evil, for Christ was with her! I remember her happy face, so pale, yet so sweet and beautiful! I remember the long black braid of hair that lay along her pillow. Then my mother, filled with the Spirit, looked up and saw clearly what we could not see. I have never forgotten it: "I can see Jesus and my baby now!" Then she closed her eyes, and her body went to sleep; but the angels carried her straight Home to the bosom of God. She could now hold her dear baby who preceded her, to her heart again! Mother recognized Jesus. More than that, she recognized her baby. I am sure that instantly in Heaven she recognized every saint.

Multitudes of other dying saints have given their brief testimonies.

My stepmother's father sang on his deathbed. He heard the sweet voices of angels and recognized his wife who had preceded him to Glory. In that brief time when the gates of Glory are left ajar to receive them and before they breathe the last breath, dying saints recognize inhabitants of Glory.

Thank God, we shall know each other in Heaven! Heavenly recognition is proved by the Bible and witnessed by the blessed testimonies of those who have looked within the gates.

5—In Heaven They Observe Us on Earth With Complete Knowledge and Eager Interest

After my mother died, one evening my sister and I sat out in the moonlight on the stone doorstep of Aunt Nannie's home and looked up at the stars. We talked about mother—did she look down upon us? Did she care? Did she still love us? We wondered upon what bright star or whether on the pale yet brilliant moon our mother was happy with the Lord.

No doubt the same questions, too deep for childish minds to put into words, have raised themselves in millions of hearts.

Do our loved ones in Heaven know what goes on on the earth? I can say with assurance and prove by the Word of God that they do know, that they do care!

Some thoughtless one will answer, "How could a mother in Heaven be happy if she knew her son on earth went on in sin, rejecting Christ, and perhaps knew that he died unconverted and went to Hell? How could people in Heaven be happy if they knew all the sadness and wickedness, all the disease, crime and failure, all the war, divorce and sin of this poor, wicked world?"

But another question will answer this one: How can

the Lord Jesus in Heaven be happy? Surely He knows all things here. He looked into Hell and heard the cries of the rich man tormented in flame. And He, with God the Father, knows the fall of every sparrow and numbers every hair on every head. He looks at the heart of every unrepentant sinner and grieves at the mistakes and failures of every Christian. Can Jesus be happy in Heaven?

The Scripture answers: "He shall see of the travail of his soul, and shall be satisfied" (Isa. 53:11). We know that Jesus on earth looked forward to the joy in Heaven, for we are told: "Who for the joy that was set before him endured the cross, despising the shame, and is set down at the right hand of the throne of God" (Heb. 12:2). Yes, Jesus, knowing all the wickedness of this world, is happy in Heaven. So are the saints in Heaven.

The trouble with all these doubters is simply that they are measuring saints in Heaven by the standards of poor, carnal, earth-minded Christians. I am burdened for sinners to be saved, yet the joy of the Lord sometimes fills my soul even here on earth. So much more will it be so when I shall awake in His likeness!

Dear Christian, you may be sure that when you get to Heaven you will be perfectly satisfied and happy with everything the Lord Jesus does.

And when, at the last judgment, He sends sinners away forever to the lake of fire, unrepentant sinners, sinners who would have nothing to do with Jesus, sinners who rejected the pleading of the Spirit, sinners who trampled under their feet the blood, then every mother will say "Amen" to the just condemnation of her boy. Then every wife will be comforted concerning her husband who would not be saved. God Himself shall wipe away all tears, and there will be no more crying or sighing or pain, "for the former things are passed away."

Certainly in Heaven they know what goes on here on earth. That is made clear by many scriptural illustrations.

There is the case of Samuel who died. King Saul, backslidden and out of the will of God, went to the witch of Endor and asked that Samuel might be brought back to advise him. Since witchcraft and spiritualism were forbidden of God, I do not know why God allowed Samuel to appear in person to Saul, but He did. Perhaps God worked it all together to suit Himself without the witch. Certainly she seemed startled when she saw Samuel. Returning Samuel, who had already gone to Heaven, knew just what was happening on earth. In fact, he knew more: he knew what would happen on the morrow. First Samuel 28:16-19 tells us what Samuel said to Saul:

"Then said Samuel, Wherefore then dost thou ask of me, seeing the Lord is departed from thee, and is become thine enemy? And the Lord hath done to him, as he spake by me: for the Lord hath rent the kingdom out of thine hand, and given it to thy neighbour, even to David: Because thou obeyedst not the voice of the Lord, nor executedst his fierce wrath upon Amalek, therefore hath the Lord done this thing unto thee this day. Moreover the Lord will also deliver Israel with thee into the hand of the Philistines: and to morrow shalt thou and thy sons be with me: the Lord also shall deliver the host of Israel into the hand of the Philistines."

Samuel knew what went on on earth, and knew why. He knew the sin of Saul, knew the purposes of God, knew what would happen on the morrow. Surely this is evidence that saints in Glory know what goes on on the earth.

The rich man in Hell looked with the deepest concern upon the affairs of the earth and said, "I pray thee therefore, father, that thou wouldst send him to my father's house: for I have five brethren; that he may testify unto them, lest they also come into this place of torment." He knew that his brethren had not repented. Abraham in Heaven knew more about it than the rich man did and said, "If they hear not Moses and the prophets, neither will they be persuaded, though one rose from the dead."

How strange that both Heaven and Hell look on with such intense concern for the conversion of the wicked here on earth while we who have an opportunity to warn them do so little about it!

When Moses and Elijah met Jesus on the Mount of Transfiguration, what do you suppose they talked about? Did Jesus speak with longing concerning the glories of Heaven for which He was homesick? Did Moses tell Him of sweet conversations in Heaven? Did Elijah report on the songs they sang and their praises?

No. These saints from Glory "spake of his decease which he should accomplish at Jerusalem" (Luke 9:31). The saints in Heaven knew what Jesus was doing on earth, knew the course of events that led straight to the cross. Eagerly they talked with the Lord about His death that He would "accomplish" (not a death that would overcome Him unwillingly) in Jerusalem.

Can't you see that in Heaven they know what goes on on earth?

"And when he had opened the fifth seal, I saw under the altar the souls of them that were slain for the word of God, and for the testimony which they held: And they cried with a loud voice, saying, How long, O Lord,

holy and true, dost thou not judge and avenge our blood on them that dwell on the earth? And white robes were given unto every one of them; and it was said unto them, that they should rest yet for a little season, until their fellowservants also and their brethren, that should be killed as they were, should be fulfilled."— Rev. 6:9-11.

Here John saw the souls in Heaven, the souls of those that had been slain because of their Christian testimony. They had not yet received resurrection bodies; but gathered below the altar of the temple in Heaven they cried out, "How long, O Lord, holy and true, dost thou not judge and avenge our blood on them that dwell on the earth?"

When saints in Heaven see the war, the persecution of Christians, the injustice, the wickedness on every hand, their poor hearts cry out that sin be punished and that saints be avenged by the hand of God.

These in Heaven look on with great concern and see the course of events in this world. But, thank God, they are not left in ignorance nor in grief. "And white robes were given unto every one of them; and it was said unto them, that they should rest yet for a little season, until their fellowservants also and their brethren, that should be killed as they were, should be fulfilled" (Rev. 6:11).

God tenderly explains to the saints in Glory how things will turn out here on earth. Heavenly instructors show them that they need not grieve, that in the end sin will be punished, right will be rewarded and Christ will reign!

Let us praise God that the souls of the saints in Heaven look down upon us here on earth with the deepest concern. As Abraham and Lazarus knew about the rich man in Hell, and as the souls in Heaven knew about the course of events on earth, so our beloved dead who are alive in Christ know what we do here day by day.

And what is the chief concern of the saints in Heaven? Is it hard for you to know? We may be sure their interest is just the same as the Saviour's. His concern is chiefly for souls to be saved. Remember that Jesus said, "I say unto you, that likewise joy shall be in heaven over one sinner that repenteth, more than over ninety and nine just persons, which need no repentance" (Luke 15:7).

And again He said, "Likewise, I say unto you, there is joy in the presence of the angels of God over one sinner that repenteth" (vs. 10).

Who is in the presence of the angels? The Lord Jesus and He rejoices over souls saved. But remember that there, too, are the saints. They are with Christ. The angels are their ministering spirits. It was the angels who carried them there to Heaven. And I think that Jesus meant that redeemed saints in Glory shout with rejoicing and praise God over every sinner who repents on earth!

In Hebrews, chapter 11, God gives us an honor roll of the heroes of faith: "By faith Abel . . .," "By faith Enoch . . .," "By faith Noah . . .," "By faith Abraham . . .," etc., with Isaac and Jacob and Sara and Gideon and Barak and Samson and Jephthae and unnamed martyrs of the faith of whom the world was not worthy! Then the wonderful climax of the passage is found in Hebrews 12:1,2:

"Wherefore seeing we also are compassed about with so great a cloud of witnesses, let us lay aside every weight, and the sin which doth so easily beset us, and let us run with patience the race that is set before us,

Looking unto Jesus the author and finisher of our faith . . . ."

The word WITNESSES here might mean that these are martyrs who testify to us. But in view of the fact that they are said to compass us about, and in view of the many other Scriptures that teach on this point, we may be sure that all the saints and heroes of God cluster around the banisters of Heaven and gaze with the deepest concern upon us who are left here to run our race! And the force of the argument is that, since the grandstand of Glory is filled with so many eager observers, we should lay aside every sin and the besetting sin of unbelief and look to Jesus to complete (finish) our faith, and we should run our race with patience.

These sainted millions have run their race; they have fought their fight; they have finished their course. Now they watch on the sidelines as we take their places. O Christians, in view of this multitude who compass us about and watch us, let us run a good race!

Heavenly saints know what goes on here on earth. They know as Jesus knows. They see, not through a glass darkly, but face to face. God has no secrets from His beloved who are entered into His presence and rejoice in His courts.

My thoughts recur again and again to my mother. I never knew until I was a grown man that she had wanted me to be a preacher. One day in Amarillo, Texas, in the home of my dear Aunt Essie, mother's sister, we were looking through an old book, and a letter fell out. I recognized the handwriting at once, for I had seen her maidenhood's love letters to my father. The handwriting was that of my mother, written when I was four years old, a year or two before her death.

She wrote, as mothers will, about husband and children. Her baby (who soon preceded her to Heaven) was doing better, she thought. Gertrude, the older girl, was good to help mama in drying dishes and minding the baby, she said. Ruth, with her blond curls, was very quiet and sweet; George, my younger brother, was into mischief from morning to night! Then she said, "And my little preacher boy is just getting along fine. The other day he said. . . ."

Startled, I looked up at my aunt. She had named everybody else but me! I was her "preacher boy"! "Did she call me that?" I asked. Aunt Essie answered, "She never called you anything else!"

When I saw my father a little later, I mentioned the incident. Very gravely he said, "Yes, when you were born we gave you to God and prayed that He would make you a preacher." I remembered then that when I was four I had been taught to answer, when people asked me my name, "I am John the Baptist preacher!"

"Why didn't you tell me, dad?" I asked. He replied, "We wanted the Lord to tell you!" The Lord did tell me, and I know now that to this end was I born.

The burdens of the ministry are heavy enough sometimes, God knows. There is more to be done than any one man can do. And any true preacher must lose friends for the sake of the bold, plain message that he preaches. There are tasks too heavy for any mortal. Then there is, or ought to be, the unceasing pain in the heart which Paul felt for his brethren, the Jews, willing to be accursed from Christ, and which we must feel for the unsaved multitudes, unthinking, unheeding, but for whom Christ died.

Yet there are joys and recompenses so that the work is easy and the burden is light. When human power fails, there is the power of the Holy Ghost. When others forsake, there is the very real presence of Christ even to the end of the age. And there is a payday coming, more certain than Saturday night. And not the least of a Christian's joy is that joy which takes place in Heaven over a sinner saved.

Many a time I stand and plead with sinners to come to Christ, and they do, thank God, through the power of His Gospel and of the Spirit. When they come—sometimes with glad, uplifted faces, sometimes in tears—I feel that in Heaven they make way for my mother, and she gets a front seat in the grandstand of Glory. I think I can almost hear her rejoicing as she sees her prayers being answered and her boy preaching the Gospel! Then "there is joy in heaven"!

Since Heaven is so near and since such a cloud of witnesses surrounds us, let us run our race with patience, laying aside the weights and our besetting sin of unbelief. Jesus will give us the soul-winner's faith, the soul-winner's power while Heaven looks on. And one day we shall share with them the soul-winner's reward and enter more perfectly into the soul-winner's rejoicing.

It is a solemn, yet most comforting, fact that in Heaven they know what we do here on earth. Heavenly witnesses watch our every step! We are dear to them; they understand our hearts; they anxiously look for us to come Home.

If you want to cause people in Heaven to rejoice, then today trust Jesus Christ to forgive you and save you. Then all Heaven will be glad!

6—Christian, "To Die Is Gain"; We Should Long for Heaven

We Christians often act like heathen. We preach that it is wonderful to be a Christian, that Heaven is to be gained and Hell shunned. Then when one of our loved ones dies, we act as if it were all a lie. Our actions say that this world is better than the next, that death is a tragedy, and we ask querulously in our unbelief, Why? Why? Why?

We feel that Heaven is bearable, all right, when one has sucked dry all the pleasures of earth. We feel that, only after old age has come upon us, when life is a burden, when health has failed, when we are in the way and our children don't want us, then perhaps we should be resigned to go to Heaven. Subconsciously we look upon Heaven as a scrapheap for the worn-out and useless, a kind of old people's home—better than nothing but not as good as this world, with youth, health and prosperity.

Shame on us! When we weep and lament at the death of our loved ones, we often make void our testimony, cast reflection upon the Bible and irreverence on Heaven.

For the Christian, death is not a tragedy but a glorious promotion—not the sad end, but the glorious beginning.

Sometimes we hear people say how sad it is that one should die so young. But that is a deception of Satan. If a young Christian dies, it is not sad but glorious. Many of the fairest buds that ever grew on earth have blossomed in Heaven. However much we miss our loved ones when they fall asleep, let us remember that our mourning is selfish. There is rejoicing in Heaven. Not one in that blessed land would, if he could, return to the decaying form he left, to live out the life he had planned, to see the happiest future he could imagine on this earth. Death for a sinner is horrible, but never to a child of God. "Blessed are the dead which die in the Lord from henceforth: Yea, saith the Spirit, that they may rest from their labours; and their works do follow them" (Rev. 14:13). Blessed and happy are the Christian dead!

"For to me to live is Christ, and to die is gain. But if I live in the flesh, this is the fruit of my labour: yet what I shall choose I wot not. For I am in a strait betwixt two, having a desire to depart, and to be with Christ; which is far better."—Phil. 1:21-23.

To die is gain. "Having a desire to depart, and to be with Christ; which is far better," Paul said. It is gain, always gain, for a Christian to die. It is better, far better, to depart and be with Christ. Thus happy or fortunate or blessed are the dead who die in the Lord.

Then Christians should eagerly look forward to Heaven. For Jesus to come today and take away His saints, His bride, would be glorious. But if Jesus does not come today, then blessed and happy are those who die in Christ.

We ought to sing songs about Heaven, long after its beauties, rejoice because of the certainty that one glad day we shall be there. We ought to welcome the call that may come for us at any moment. We ought truly to be homesick for Heaven and willing to stay here on earth only that we may do the will of Christ and bless others in His name and work.

Let us consider the great gain of one who dies and goes to Heaven.

1. *The Christian gains the presence of Christ at death.* Paul said, "Having a desire to depart, and to be with

Christ; which is far better." He longed to see Jesus; so should we. He spoke of being "absent from the body, and . . . present with the Lord." Where Jesus is 'tis Heaven.

It is the desire of His dear heart that we who love Him should be with Him. He is now preparing a place and will come for us. "Where I am, there ye may be also."

I can never quite realize how He loves me. I know He does, for His Word tells me so, and He shows it with a multitude of mercies day by day. His Holy Spirit tells me so in my heart. Yet how sweet it will be when I can see Him in person! Then hope will change to glad fruition, faith to sight, and prayer to praise. Then I can put my finger on the nail prints and my hand in His side. Then I can hold His feet as did Mary Magdalene and the other Mary, or lean upon His bosom as did John. It will be Heaven enough to be with Jesus. If we love Him now, having never seen Him, how we must love Him when we see Him face to face!

2. *Heaven will be glorious because we will see our loved ones again.* My heart often sings the words of the old song, "I have a mother over yonder" and "I have a father over yonder." I have now many in Heaven who long to see me.

When our boys came home from the First World War, what bedlam in an Army camp when the Armistice was signed, when the nations laid down their arms and when everybody prepared to go home again to wife and mother and sweetheart and babies! I can never forget it. Surely that is only a faint picture of the joy when a saint goes Home and meets all his loved ones again. My mother committed her orphan children into the tender hands of God, unafraid and without fret, then turned her face beautifully toward Heaven.

There is coming a glad time when all the saved who ever sang, "God be with you till we meet again," will meet at Jesus' feet. The saints will "gather at the river." They will come in from the East, West, North and South and sit down with Abraham, Isaac and Jacob in the kingdom of God. Oh, it will be glorious to meet our loved ones in Heaven!

3. *Christians will be done with sin.* It was about his own sins and sinful nature that Paul cried out, "O wretched man that I am! who shall deliver me from the body of this death?" (Rom. 7:24). Then they that hunger and thirst after righteousness shall be filled. Then the pure in heart shall see God. There will be no more tears for the loved ones who died in the Lord and thus who have gone to be with Him.

4. *There will be no more grief over sinful companions.* Lot vexed his righteous soul with the unlawful deeds of the men of Sodom. With broken heart, Samuel cried to the Lord all night because of the sins of Saul and because God rejected Saul from being king. Jeremiah had a fire in his bones. Paul had unceasing pain for his brethren according to the flesh who rejected Paul's Saviour, and went on their way to Hell.

Christians in this world sadly need the admonition, "Fret not thyself because of evil doers, neither be thou envious against the workers of iniquity" (Ps. 37:1). Praise God, in Heaven there will be no sin about us, no bad companions, no persecutors! No liquor ads on restaurant menus, no taverns to pass by. None of that, for the drunkards shall not enter the kingdom of God. Here men take God's name in vain, but in Heaven the cherubim cry, "Holy, holy, holy, Lord God Almighty." So the Christian will gain in Heaven complete freedom from the sorrows of surrounding sin. How blessed to die in the Lord!

5. *Our tears will be dried and sorrowing hearts will be comforted.* Abraham said to the rich man in Hell, about Lazarus, "Now he is COMFORTED, and thou art tormented" (Luke 16:25).

The Saviour said, "Blessed are they that mourn: for they shall be comforted" (Matt. 5:4). Much of this comfort we will never receive until we get to Heaven. Truly, "weeping may endure for a night, but joy cometh in the morning" (Ps. 30:5).

When the Christian dies, he loses his sorrows. If one glistening tear can stain the pure face of a saint in Glory, then God Himself will wipe it away and comfort with His own endearments all His own who have sorrowed! Pain will be forgotten. Poverty will turn into riches!

> There's no disappointment in Heaven,
>   No weariness, sorrow or pain;
> No hearts that are bleeding and broken,
>   No song with a minor refrain.
> The clouds of our earthly horizon
>   Will never appear in the sky,
> For all will be sunshine and gladness,
>   With never a sob nor a sigh.
>
> We'll never pay rent on our mansion,
>   The taxes will never come due;
> Our garments will never grow threadbare,
>   But always be fadeless and new;
> We'll never be hungry nor thirsty,
>   Nor languish in poverty there,
> For all the rich bounties of Heaven
>   His sanctified children will share.
>
> There'll never be crepe on the doorknob,
>   No funeral train in the sky;
> No graves on the hillsides of Glory,

For there we shall never more die.
The old will be young there forever,
　Transformed in a moment of time;
Immortal we'll stand in His likeness,
　The stars and the sun to outshine.

I'm bound for that beautiful city
　My Lord has prepared for His own;
Where all the redeemed of all ages
　Sing "Glory" around the white throne;
Sometimes I grow homesick for Heaven,
　And the glories I there shall behold:
What a joy that will be when my Saviour I see,
　In that beautiful city of gold!

　　　　*(With grateful acknowledgment
　　　　to the author, F. M. Lehman)*

Let all the saints who sorrow here know that there is comfort in Heaven. "Earth has no sorrow that Heaven cannot heal." To die, a Christian gains the comfort of Heaven.

6. *A Christian who dies gains rest.* Let us not complain if here we labor. We are commanded, "Let us not be weary in well doing: for in due season we shall reap, if we faint not" (Gal. 6:9). The Lord Jesus said, "I must work the works of him that sent me, while it is day: the night cometh, when no man can work" (John 9:4). Paul declared that he was a greater apostle in that he was "in labours more abundant" (II Cor. 11:23). He labored "night and day with tears" (Acts 20:31) as he warned men both publicly and from house to house. Paul literally nearly killed himself with overwork (II Cor. 1:8).

It is shameful for a Christian worker, a preacher or soul winner, to be lazy. The harvest is white now, and we must work. But there comes a time of rest. For a Christian death means sweet rest!

This is part of the blessedness which the Scriptures promise to those who die in the Lord: "And I heard a voice from heaven saying unto me, Write, Blessed are the dead which die in the Lord from henceforth: Yea, saith the Spirit, that they may REST from their labours; and their works do follow them" (Rev. 14:13). Rest!

A dear preacher friend of mine who was suddenly killed had started to drive more than 900 miles in half a night and a day, to begin a new series of revival services. Though a young man, he was burdened with many duties, but he bore them with great joy because he wanted to make full proof of his ministry. He preached the Word, being instant in season and out of season. He endured hardness as a good soldier of Jesus Christ. But now he will never need to hurry anymore. He is resting from his labors, and his works do follow him.

How sweet it must be for a saint in Heaven to lay aside all the cares and burdens and know that his works go on!

Youth feels sometimes it will never grow tired. Youth longs for the fight, for the toil, for the challenge to strength and endurance. But after awhile one begins to grow weary, not tired OF the work, but tired IN it.

Many a preacher sometimes thinks of the time when he will sit under green trees or paddle in cool waters or meditate amid the grandeur of the mountains or by the seashore or perhaps simply rest at home with wife and children. Yet for multitudes of preachers and other Christians as well, that time never comes. The vacation time is postponed; the honeymoon trip is never taken; there is no time for the little outing or the visit to the children or the quiet rest for study and refreshment.

But all such men should look forward to the glad day

when weary hands may fold themselves. I think for tired Christians it will surely be wonderful to sit on the bank of the river of life, in the shade of trees that bear twelve manner of fruits and whose leaves are for the healing of the nations! "Yea, saith the Spirit, that they may rest from their labours"!

Dad can never lay down the burden of making a living. There are clothes to buy, rent to pay, mouths to feed, tuition to pay. Many a mother has an unceasing round of duties—no forty-hour week for her. She has no office hours—no time to be sick, no time for vacation, no time for study, no time to rest. Often enough a dear mother feels that she hardly has time to pray!

Let every tired and overburdened Christian rejoice in the comforting fact that one day he shall rest from his labors while his work goes on. Rest is part of the wonderful gain of one who dies in the Lord.

Hard labor is part of the curse put on mankind because of sin. The thorns and briars in the field, the travail and sorrow of motherhood, all the bread which mankind must eat in the sweat of his face and by unceasing labor are the fruit of sin. When God reaches down and takes one of His children out of this world of sin, then he is done with toil and finds rest from his labor.

Many a Christian has found joy in the words of the song by Herbert Buffum:

> Here so many are taking vacations,
>   To the mountains, the lakes or the sea;
> Where they rest from their cares and their worries—
>   What a wonderful time that must be!
> But it seems not my lot to be like them,
>   I must toil through the heat and the cold
> Seeking out the lost sheep on the mountains,
>   Bringing wanderers back to the fold.

Chorus—

> When I take my vacation in Heaven,
>   What a wonderful time that will be!
> Hearing concerts by the heavenly chorus,
>   And the face of my Saviour I'll see.
> Sitting down on the banks of the river,
>   'Neath the shade of the Evergreen Tree
> I shall rest from my burdens forever—
>   Won't you spend your vacation with me?

There is rest, sweet rest, in Heaven.

Of the souls under the altar in Heaven John says, "White robes were given unto every one of them; and it was said unto them, that they should rest . . ." (Rev. 6:11).

7. *To die in Christ is to gain eternal rewards.* One reason it is so blessed to die in the Lord is that then one enters into the fruit of all his labor and begins to enjoy all the treasure laid up in Heaven. No doubt this thought put the ring of glory in Paul's last cry of exultation when he wrote to Timothy:

"For I am now ready to be offered, and the time of my departure is at hand. I have fought a good fight, I have finished my course, I have kept the faith: Henceforth there is laid up for me a crown of righteousness, which the Lord, the righteous judge, shall give me at that day: and not to me only, but unto all them also that love his appearing."—II Tim. 4:6-8.

Part of the Christian's reward will be reigning with Christ when He comes in glory and when the bodies of the saints are raised. Then the twelve apostles shall sit on twelve thrones, judging the twelve tribes of Israel. Then to one Christ will say, "Thou hast been faithful in a very little, have thou authority over ten cities" (Luke 19:17). But Paul knew that when he departed to be with Christ he would have the inexpressible joy of seeing souls whom he had won come home to God. His works would follow him!

The Prophet Daniel foresaw that "they that be wise shall shine as the brightness of the firmament; and they that turn many to righteousness as the stars for ever and ever" (Dan. 12:3). Surely a part of that eternal glory and reward begins when a Christian enters Heaven.

How great gain has one who leaves earth for Heaven! Truly the Christian can say, "To die is gain," and that "to depart, and to be with Christ . . . is far better."

7—Christ May Come Today to Take His Own

Death is a door to Heaven. For that reason Paul could say, "To die is gain." Thus, "Blessed are the dead which die in the Lord." My mother could rejoice and ask for a song as she went out to meet God in that little unpainted country home in north Texas many years ago.

Death is a door to Heaven. But it is not the only door to Heaven. Millions of Christians will enter Heaven without dying. When Jesus comes, He will take all His to Heaven, and those who live to that glad day shall in a moment be caught up to meet the Lord in the air and carried straight to Heaven. Enoch and Elijah went to Heaven without dying. So will millions of others, when Jesus comes.

In John 14 the Saviour comforted His disciples before they went to the Garden of Gethsemane and talked to them about Heaven. "And if I go and prepare a place for you, I will come again, and receive you unto myself; that where I am, there ye may be also."

We need not necessarily think of death in connection with Heaven. Death is a way to Heaven but not the main way. Throughout the Bible the Christian is taught to look forward to the day when Jesus comes and when he will be taken to Heaven without dying.

There are some who foolishly teach that, when Jesus said, "I will come again, and receive you unto myself," He spoke of death. But He did not. Others say that, when Jesus said, "I will come again," He spoke of the coming of the Holy Spirit. But that is not what He said, nor meant. Jesus plainly said, "*I* will come again."

When Jesus stood on the Mount of Olives just outside Jerusalem and gave His last message to the disciples and was then taken up into Heaven and a cloud received Him out of their sight, two heavenly messengers came and stood by them and said, "Ye men of Galilee, why stand ye gazing up into heaven? this same Jesus, which is taken up from you into heaven, shall so come in like manner as ye have seen him go into heaven" (Acts 1:11).

The same Jesus is coming again. His going away was literal, physical, bodily. His return will be just as literal. Jesus went away to prepare a place for all the born-again and redeemed children of God. The same Jesus is coming back again to receive them. Jesus said, "And if I go and prepare a place for you, I will come again, and receive you unto myself; that where I am, there ye may be also."

Those who are in Christ and alive when Jesus comes to receive His own will be changed in a moment and will never die, but will be carried straight to Heaven.

In I Corinthians 15:51,52, we are told what will happen when Jesus comes for His saints:

"Behold, I shew you a mystery; We shall not all sleep, but we shall all be changed, In a moment, in the twinkling of an eye, at the last trump: for the trumpet shall sound, and the dead shall be raised incorruptible, and we shall be changed."

SLEEP is God's way of speaking about DEATH for the child of God. But "we shall all be changed." Not all Christians will die. Not all of us will leave this body and have it buried in a grave. Not all of us shall be carried out to the cemeteries. Not all of us shall say good-by to weeping loved ones while the flickering breath of life leaves us. We shall not all sleep.

It is not true that every Christian will die. When Jesus comes, all the saved will be changed in a moment, in the twinkling of an eye at that trumpet sound. The Christian dead shall be raised up with immortal, incorruptible bodies, and Christians who are alive will be changed and given immortal, glorified bodies immediately.

So every Christian should hope that Jesus will come for and take us away to the heavenly mansions He has prepared before death comes.

After all, it matters little, just so we go straight to Heaven. And the Christians who have gone on before will return with Christ to get resurrected bodies from the graves. Look at I Thessalonians 4:13-18:

"But I would not have you to be ignorant, brethren, concerning them which are asleep, that ye sorrow not, even as others which have no hope. For if we believe that Jesus died and rose again, even so them also which sleep in Jesus will God bring with him. For this we say unto you by the word of the Lord, that we which are alive and remain unto the coming of the Lord shall

not prevent them which are asleep. For the Lord himself shall descend from heaven with a shout, with the voice of the archangel, and with the trump of God: and the dead in Christ shall rise first: Then we which are alive and remain shall be caught up together with them in the clouds, to meet the Lord in the air: and so shall we ever be with the Lord. Wherefore comfort one another with these words."

Jesus is coming back to get His own. When He comes, those of His whose bodies sleep in graves will come back with Jesus to receive those bodies. The bodies will be raised up from the graves first; then we Christians "which are alive and remain shall be caught up together with them in the clouds, to meet the Lord in the air."

The saved who are already in Heaven will come back with Jesus to meet us. Their bodies will rise out of the graves; then we shall be changed, and together we shall meet Christ up in the air and then go with Him to the Father's house of many mansions for our honeymoon in Heaven!

Then we shall see again all of our loved ones in Christ. Then aches, pains, partings will be forever past. Oh, what a meeting when we are caught up in the air to meet all our loved ones whose bodies will be raised out of the graves and whose spirits will come back from Heaven; and the dear Lord Jesus will fulfill His promise: "I will come again, and receive you unto myself; that where I am, there ye may be also." Blessed, blessed hope!

No one knows just when that will be. He said no man knows, "no, not the angels of heaven, but my Father only" (Matt. 24:36). Yet we know that He may come at any moment. Again and again Jesus warned His disciples to be always on the watch, that He might return at any time. Read these passages and see for yourself how many warnings there are.

"Watch therefore: for ye know not what hour your Lord doth come."—Matt. 24:42.

"Therefore be ye also ready: for in such an hour as ye think not the Son of man cometh."—Matt. 24:44.

"Watch therefore, for ye know neither the day nor the hour wherein the Son of man cometh."—Matt. 25:13.

"Take ye heed, watch and pray: for ye know not when the time is. For the Son of man is as a man taking a far journey, who left his house, and gave authority to his servants, and to every man his work, and commanded the porter to watch. Watch ye therefore: for ye know not when the master of the house cometh, at even, or at midnight, or at the cockcrowing, or in the morning: Lest coming suddenly he find you sleeping. And what I say unto you I say unto all, Watch."—Mark 13:33-37.

Since it is clear that Jesus may come at any moment, then every Christian should be continually on the watch.

Paul constantly looked forward to the coming of the Saviour in the hope that he would be caught up alive to meet the Lord in the air. In this hope, he was simply following the express command of Jesus and watching for His coming.

Paul wrote in I Corinthians 15:52, "The dead shall be raised incorruptible, and we shall be changed." He counted himself with those who would be alive and changed instantly when Jesus came. Likewise in I Thessalonians

4:15 he wrote, "we which are alive and remain unto the coming of the Lord shall not prevent them which are asleep." Paul expected to be among those alive and remaining on the earth when Jesus came. That was what Jesus had commanded Christians to look forward to, and Paul obeyed.

So a Christian ought always to look forward to the coming of the Saviour. In the epistle to Titus we are admonished to be "looking for that blessed hope, and the glorious appearing of the great God and our Saviour Jesus Christ." Blessed hope! Jesus is coming to receive us into the House of many mansions which He has prepared for us.

Through the years some have gone to Heaven. Saints have laid down their tired bodies, and their spirits have been taken Home to God. The bodies have been laid away to sleep in the dust of the earth until Jesus comes.

But one day when Jesus comes into the air to receive us, there will be a great resurrection of the bodies of the Christian dead; their spirits He will bring back with Him from Heaven; then all of us who are saved and are alive shall be changed in a moment and caught up with them to meet the Lord Jesus, and what a triumphant procession it will be as we enter Heaven!

It may be at morn, when the day is awaking,
When sunlight through darkness and shadow is breaking,
That Jesus will come in the fullness of glory,
To receive from the world "His own."

It may be at midday, it may be at twilight,
It may be, perchance, that the blackness of midnight
Will burst into light in the blaze of His glory,
When Jesus receives "His own."

While its hosts cry Hosanna, from Heaven descending,
With glorified saints and the angels attending,

With grace on His brow, like a halo of glory,
Will Jesus receive "His own."

Oh, joy! oh, delight! should we go without dying,
No sickness, no sadness, no dread and no crying,
Caught up through the clouds with our Lord into glory,
When Jesus receives "His own."

Chorus—

O Lord Jesus, how long, how long
'Ere we shout the glad song,
Christ returneth! Hallelujah!
Hallelujah! Amen, Hallelujah! Amen.

—*H. L. Turner*

When will Jesus come? No one knows. Surely Jesus may come soon. And when He comes, He will take all who have trusted in Him, all who have been born again, straight to Heaven. We shall be changed in a moment, in the twinkling of an eye. All the taint of sin will be taken away, all the frailty of body, all the weakness of the flesh. Glorified beings with sinless, immortal, deathless bodies, we shall be caught up to meet Jesus and, with a glad reunion, go straight with Him to the Father's house of many mansions.

Let us talk and think about Heaven. But oh, let us not worry nor fret about death. Likely multitudes who read this book will never die but will experience the glad quick change when the trumpet sounds and Jesus comes for His own.

Jesus said these precious words, "And if I go and prepare a place for you, I will come again, and receive you unto myself; that where I am, there ye may be also." Let us believe this precious promise. Let us memorize it, hide it in our hearts.

Jesus will come soon to take to Heaven all those who

have trusted Him as Saviour. No sickness, no dying, no funeral parlors, no graveyards, no parting from a single loved one who is saved. We shall leave all the unconverted, but all who have trusted Jesus for salvation will go to Heaven, that sweet home of the Lord Jesus and departed saints.

8—Christ the Way to Heaven; Make Sure You Are Going There

How to get to Heaven is the question that has burdened men's hearts in every clime and every age since Adam sinned. Every heathen religion has its heaven of some kind, a place of blessedness hereafter, to be earnestly desired and sought for. Whether it is called "The Happy Hunting Ground" or "Nirvana" or something else, men long for Heaven.

To make sure of gaining Heaven men have brought gifts to witch doctors, made sacrifices to their gods, paid money to priests and tortured themselves with unspeakable pains. Men have offered their sons into the fiery iron arms of Moloch; women have thrown their babies to the crocodiles of the Ganges River, hoping to gain Heaven.

Pilgrims have traversed burning deserts to bow at Mecca; crusaders have fought their way to Jerusalem to gain the assurance of peace and forgiveness hereafter. The fasting vigils of monks in their cells, the deeds of penitents who climbed stone stairs on bare knees and the millions of prayers, Ave Marias or Paternosters counted on rosary beads have been with a hope of gaining Heaven.

Men seek a way to Heaven in the waters of baptism,

in the confessional box or in the bread and wine of the Lord's Supper. They seek Heaven by lodge rites, by giving gifts to the poor, by righteous deeds. Every human heart longs to make sure of blessedness and peace and happiness hereafter.

BUT NOT ONE OF THESE IS THE WAY TO HEAVEN!

When Jesus in chapter 14 of John assured His disciples of the many mansions in His Father's House that He was preparing for His dear ones, He said, "And whither I go ye know, and the way ye know." I am glad that Thomas was there, for the doubt he expressed that day has clouded many another heart since. Jesus answered us as He answered Thomas. Thomas said, "Lord, we know not whither thou goest; and how can we know the way?" He wanted to know the way to Heaven! Jesus answered back, "I am the way, the truth, and the life: no man cometh unto the Father, but by me."

Jesus Himself is the way to Heaven. The so-called Christian Scientists (with the doctrine that denies sin, and so cannot be scientific, and denies the Bible, so cannot be Christian) call Jesus "The Way-shower." But that name does not give Christ His due. Jesus is not the Way-shower; He is the Way. No man ever came to the Father but by Him.

Men would like to take themselves to Heaven or like to have the church take them to Heaven. They would like to have their good deeds or their prayers or their alms to the poor pay their way. But that is not God's way. Jesus Himself is the only way. He is the "strait gate," the "narrow way." Every other way leads to destruction.

Jesus repeatedly said that He is the way to salvation, the way to Heaven. He said in John 7:37, "If any man thirst, let him come unto ME, and drink." He said in

Matthew 11:28, "Come unto ME, all ye that labour and are heavy laden, and I will give you rest." True rest, true salvation, true forgiveness are not found by membership in a church nor by baptism nor by righteous living. They are found only in Christ.

Peter summed up the Old Testament when he said to Cornelius and his household, "To him give all the prophets witness, that through his name whosoever believeth in him shall receive remission of sins" (Acts 10:43). That is what Paul and Barnabas preached at Antioch in Pisidia: "Be it known unto you therefore, men and brethren, that through this man is preached unto you the forgiveness of sins: And by him all that believe are justified from all things, from which ye could not be justified by the law of Moses" (Acts 13:38, 39).

God has given salvation to men. He has given us eternal life. God wants Heaven to be filled with the redeemed. But this gift of everlasting life is given through His Son. "This is the record, that God hath given to us eternal life, and this life is in his Son. He that hath the Son hath life; and he that hath not the Son of God hath not life" (I John 5:11,12).

Today if you have Jesus, you have salvation. If you have Christ, you have the way to Heaven.

Christ died to open the way to Heaven. His blood poured out on Calvary paid for man's sins. When Jesus died, the veil of the Temple was torn in two from the top to the bottom. God the Father gave Jesus to die, and in the death of His Son every barrier between man and God was torn down. Now whosoever will, may come for pardon and salvation and come safely home to Heaven.

The same Jesus who died rose again. His death paid

for sin. He is now our High Priest. He died for our sins. He arose for our justification. Everything about salvation Jesus did.

Now the same Jesus who died to prepare sinners for Heaven has gone to prepare Heaven for forgiven sinners! "I go to prepare a place for you. And if I go and prepare a place for you, I will come again, and receive you unto myself; that where I am, there ye may be also" (John 14:2,3). He died and rose to prepare sinners for Heaven. He is now preparing Heaven for saved sinners, and one day He is coming to take redeemed sinners to Himself in Heaven. That is what He said to His disciples.

Can't you see that there is no way any man could reach Heaven except through Christ alone?

Now the way to Heaven is open. The blood has already been shed. Jesus did it Himself. When He died, He said, "It is finished." The way to Heaven is finished. The price for sin is finished. Soon the preparation of Heaven itself will be finished, and Christ will come for all His blood-bought and blood-washed ones.

Can't you see that the Lord Jesus has opened the way and all who will, may go to Heaven?

How can a man today make sure of Heaven? Not by his good deeds, for that is not the way. Not by joining the church and being baptized, for the church is not the way. Rites and ceremonies are not the way. Being good is not the way to Heaven. The only way to make sure of Heaven is to receive Jesus Christ as your personal Saviour, receive Him as the One who died for you, the One who is the way to Heaven. Salvation is a free gift.

You remember that Jesus said in John 6:37, "Him that cometh to ME I will in no wise cast out." Won't you today come to Him in your heart? The Bible says, "Whosoever shall call upon the name of the Lord shall be saved" (Rom. 10:13). Jesus said, "Behold, I stand at the door and knock: if any man hear my voice, and open the door, I will come in" (Rev. 3:20). You have only to open the door and let Jesus in; then you are sure of Heaven.

God meant the same thing in John 1:12: "But as many as received him [Jesus], to them gave he power to become the sons of God, even to them that believe on his name." If today you will receive Him, simply open your heart and trust Him to come in; then He will give you the power to become the child of God and guarantee you a home in Heaven.

You can be sure of Heaven.

Yesterday evening I sat on the front porch of a very humble little home. There live an elderly couple, their only support a few dollars a month. Yet they sat and praised God with me. As I sang, "No Disappointment in Heaven," they wept for joy and praised God aloud.

They are perfectly content to stay, yet eager to go. The man, a saint of nearly eighty years, told me of the glad assurance he has that Heaven is his home. In the midst of His praises he placed his hand over his heart and said, "I have talked too much. My heart is weak."

One of these days very soon that old heart will stop beating, and the angels will carry my dear brother straight to Heaven. Yet as he talked about it there was no grief, no doubt, no fear, only a glad faith, a glorious expectation.

You, too, can have that perfect assurance by simply trusting Christ for forgiveness. Receive Him into your heart; then rest your soul upon Him who said, "Him that cometh to me I will in no wise cast out."

Jesus Himself is the way to Heaven; and if you will trust Him to take you there, your soul will be safe for eternity.

Perhaps some reader has lost a little baby by the hand of death. It may be that you are troubled, wondering whether the little one is in Heaven.

I am glad to tell you on the authority of the Word of God that every little child who dies while he is an unaccountable sinner, dies before conscious sin, is taken immediately to Heaven. It is true that every child born into the world is tainted by the sinful nature he inherits from all preceding generations. But the Lord Jesus Christ has made atonement for even that sinful nature. All that a little baby has lost by Adam's sin and the curse on the whole race, Christ has purchased back for him. Read I Corinthians 15:22: "For as in Adam all die, even so in Christ shall all be made alive."

No one goes to Hell because of Adam's sin. Christ has paid for that for every unaccountable baby. It is only by conscious sin, sin by choice, that children become lost sinners. How early in life that is, we do not know. Doubtless it is much earlier with some children than with others.

Five of my six girls claimed Christ and gave sweet evidence of a real change of heart before they were six. If carefully taught and trained, children may be led to Christ while very young. But all who have not yet come to know themselves sinners, and so have become accountable to God, are kept safe. And when a baby dies, dear Jesus takes the little one to Heaven at once.

King David's baby died, but God revealed to David that

he could see his little one again in Heaven. David said, "I shall go to him, but he shall not return to me" (II Sam. 12:23).

Dear mother with the empty arms and aching heart; dear father who has followed the hearse out to the silent City of the Dead and buried the mortal body of the baby you loved so well, and with him, perhaps, buried your dreams, air castles and plans that only the dear God knew—beloved and troubled ones, you can see your baby again if you will only trust Christ as your Saviour.

Near Hastings, Minnesota, I was taken by a good man to visit his neighbor on a big island in the Mississippi River. The bereaved man was said to be calloused and hardened, even claiming to be an infidel and a denier of the Bible. Then I learned that his little one, not over two or three years old, had fallen into the waters and drowned. When I began to talk about the little one, his hard heart melted and eagerly he began to ask me if God had sent his baby to Hell! He had a Catholic background, and the little one had not been sprinkled. Was she, then, lost forever?

But I showed him II Samuel 12:23 and I Corinthians 15:22, making plain that all the sins of the world must be borne by Jesus Christ on the cross and showing how God is anxious to forgive them all. I showed him that God does not charge them against unaccountable babies and is so anxious for every poor sinner to trust Christ for forgiveness and a new heart.

Then all the suspicion of preachers, all the rebellion against the churches, all the doubt about God and the Bible were gone! With a contrite heart and trembling lips, the man who had lost his baby girl agreed to pray.

We bowed our heads by the car, and he apparently confessed his sin to Christ and trusted Him for mercy and forgiveness!

Who knows but that God took your baby in order to turn your heart to Heaven also? Anyone who is capable of reading this is mature enough to realize himself to be a sinner. You are not an unaccountable infant. You have CHOSEN wrong when you knew what was right. You know you need a Saviour. Jesus is the One who can take you to Heaven. Trust Him today to forgive your sins and change your heart and make you sure of Heaven!

Some of you have lost loved ones. Perhaps they were not perfect—who ever was, save Jesus Christ alone? They did not keep all the commandments, just as you have not and as I have not. Were they saved? Can you have assurance of seeing them in the glad land where sin never comes, where people never grow old, where there is no dying and no parting?

I tell you gladly that if you are saved you can see them again. They are safe in Heaven if they committed their souls to Jesus Christ in simple faith and accepted Him as Saviour.

Perhaps the one you have in mind did not do what God said about baptism. The dying thief was not baptized. Perhaps you think of many things they left undone. So will our loved ones have to admit when we are gone that we failed. No one ever got to Heaven by deserving it. The only way to Heaven is this way: Christ died for sinners, and all who trust Him have salvation and everlasting life! "For God so loved the world, that he gave his only begotten Son, that whosoever believeth in him should not perish, but have everlasting life" (John 3:16).

Those who love Christ and have trusted Him for salvation ought to try to please Him every day. When we see Jesus, we shall be ashamed of every bad influence or motive, and we shall miss a reward. Oh, it is important to live for Christ earnestly, and He will gloriously reward us for our labors.

But rewards are one thing, and salvation is entirely another. The way to Heaven is not by good works but by trusting in Jesus Christ alone for forgiveness and eternal salvation. Not one single person was ever worthy of salvation. You must accept salvation as a free gift, undeserved, or never be saved.

God is ready. Christ has prepared a home for you in Heaven. He wants you there. I believe you want to go there. Then put your trust in Jesus Christ now and have it settled forever that you will expect Him to take you to the mansion He has prepared for you.

Suppose you shut the door and get down on your knees and tell Jesus Christ that you will trust Him now to be your Saviour, trust Him to forgive all your sins, trust Him to change your heart and risk Him to take you Home to Heaven. Or sitting in that chair or lying in that bed— wherever you are, right now trust Him with all your heart. The moment you wholly depend on Him you have everlasting life.

Now if you would make sure of Heaven today and will receive Christ as your Saviour and trust Him to forgive all your sins and take you straight Home at last, suppose you write it down right here. Can you sign this statement honestly? If you can, it will be a witness to you and to others and will give assurance to your heart.

My Decision for Christ and Heaven

Here and now I confess myself a sinner. I trust Jesus Christ to save me as He promised to do. I have read this book on Heaven. I want to go there, so I now solemnly commit myself into the keeping of Jesus Christ and trust Him to take me safely Home to Heaven when Jesus comes or at death.

Signed _____ Date _____

Others may sign also if they, too, sincerely trust Christ for forgiveness and salvation and for a home in Heaven.

Signed_____

Signed_____

Signed_____

If you have trusted Christ as your Saviour and would like to let us know, why not write in a letter or a postcard about as follows:

Sword of the Lord
P. O. Box 1099
Murfreesboro, TN 37133

Dear Sword of the Lord:

Since reading your booklet on Heaven, I have confessed to Christ that I am a sinner and have trusted Him to save me. I believe He has saved me and I expect to meet you in Heaven.

Your brother (or sister) in Christ,

Signed _____

Address_____